Confidence Hacks:
99 Small Actions to
Massively
Boost Your Confidence

Barrie Davenport

Disclaimer

Your Free Gift

As a way of saying thanks for your purchase, I hope you'll enjoy "110 Empowering Essentials for a Confident Life" to help you determine where you can make positive changes for improvement and growth. Being a confident person involves all aspects of your life from your relationships to your career. The key is to identify what you want to change in each area and create a plan of action to kickstart a real positive shift.

In "110 Empowering Essentials for a Confident Life," I offer dozens of suggested actions in each life area to inspire you toward action. Becoming a more confident person doesn't happen by itself. You can boost your confidence by recognizing the behavior of confident people, and then putting those into action in your own life.

Download this free report by going to:
http://simpleselfconfidence.com/free.

Contents

Introduction

*"Action is a great restorer and builder of confidence.
Inaction is not only the result, but the cause, of fear."*

~ Norman Vincent Peale

Action is the cure for low confidence. Unfortunately, low confidence has a tendency to immobilize us. When you doubt yourself and your abilities, the last thing you want to do is put yourself out there to fall flat on your face. It's much easier to remain in the safe confines of the status quo and not expose yourself to the possibility of failure or rejection.

There's a reason your confidence has taken a hit. It could be a legitimate reason, like recently getting fired or suffering from acute shyness. Or it could be some relatively minor event from the past that no longer applies to you—but it has grown to monstrous proportions in your mind, and you keep feeding this monster with negative thoughts.

Either way, your immediate or distant past doesn't define you now or your future potential. Change and growth are always possible when you're motivated and determined, regardless of your past, your personality, or your self-perceptions. If you want to be confident, you can be—if you're willing to take action. And not just one action or a few actions, but repeated actions until fear and doubt no longer have a grip on you.

All success begins with thought and culminates in action. It is possible action will result in failure, but inaction always leads to nothing—guaranteed. An essential component of confidence is the ability to be comfortable with the uncertainty of action and the sting of failure. Failure *will* happen on occasion. Sometimes it happens many times.

Abraham Lincoln had two business ventures fail, lost eight different elections, and had a complete nervous breakdown before becoming president. Thomas Edison, who has 1,093 US patents to his name, was told by a teacher that he was too stupid to learn anything. He performed nearly 10,000 failed experiments before creating the first successful light bulb. Michael Jordan was cut from his high school basketball team for a "lack of skill." Even after becoming a pro, he says he missed more than 9,000 shots, lost almost 300 games, and missed the game-winning shots twenty-six times.

More than likely, Abraham Lincoln, Thomas Edison, and Michael Jordan went through periods of low self-confidence. But instead of letting failure completely derail them, they tried again and again and again. They took action and learned from their failures, re-calibrated their efforts, and eventually claimed success. Failure is a temporary state, fraught with potential and opportunity—but only if you get up off the ground, dust yourself off, and start moving again.

The fear of failure and rejection is the only thing standing between you and confidence. The only way to beat that fear is to take action on the very thing you that holds you back. It doesn't take much action in the beginning. Small, manageable actions in the direction of your goals and dreams are enough to get the ball rolling. Every successful small action will give you an immediate boost of confidence to try again. Even setbacks can show you the value of action and reinforce your ability to break through inertia and fear.

I've created this book to help you take small and manageable actions to jumpstart your confidence in ten different areas of your life. You may not lack confidence in all of these areas, but the actions can further cement your existing confidence and provide skills you can utilize for related situations that arise in the future. You never know when you might step into the quicksand of insecurity and doubt and need some tools to help pull you out.

I encourage you to read through the entire book once, making notes about the ideas and actions that apply to you and your difficulties with confidence. Then go back to these specific areas, prioritize them, and begin working through the recommended Action Steps. You may find the actions for one area help boost your confidence in another.

As Abraham Lincoln reminds, "You can have anything you want—if you want it badly enough. You can be anything you want to be, do anything you set out to accomplish if you hold to that desire with singleness of purpose." If confidence is your purpose, offer no more power or energy to thoughts and behaviors of self-doubt and fear. Take action now, and become the person you want to be.

Who Am I?

My name is Barrie Davenport, and I run two top-ranked personal development sites, Live Bold and Bloom and BarrieDavenport.com. I'm a certified personal coach, former public relations professional, author, and creator of several online courses on self-confidence, life passion, and habit creation.

My work as a coach, blogger, and author is focused on offering people practical strategies for living happier, more successful, more confident lives. I utilize time-tested, evidence based, action-oriented principles and methods to create real and measurable results for self-improvement.

As a coach, I've learned through countless sessions with courageous, motivated clients that each individual has the answers within them. Every person has the wisdom and intuition to know what is best for themselves. Sometimes we simply need someone or something to coax it out of us and encourage us to move forward.

That's what I hope this book will do for you—help you to move forward to a confident life where you become the best version of yourself, enjoy the success you want to achieve, and live to your fullest potential. Thank you for choosing my book to support you on your journey.

Relationships

*"To grow in our ability to love ourselves
we need to receive love as well."*

~ John Gray

When asked on their deathbeds what they most regretted during their lives, dying people consistently expressed one of their top regrets was not spending more time with family and friends. Your close relationships are the most important aspect of your life, and relationships are a vital component to good health and general well-being.

Studies show healthy relationships help you cope better with stress, feel healthier and more satisfied with life, and even live longer. Through relationships with other human beings, you grow and evolve—and you deepen and expand your experience of love and meaning.

When you aren't confident in your ability to create or sustain a healthy relationship, you undermine your confidence in every other area of your life. In fact, having positive interactions with those around you is the cornerstone for success and happiness in nearly all other life pursuits—from your career to your social life.

Your romantic relationship is the laboratory for understanding more about yourself, as well as learning valuable life skills.

Whether you're in a long-term relationship or just dating, your relationship confidence is vital to your self-esteem and the way your partner perceives you. If you don't feel confident in your ability to connect, communicate, and interact with others, improving your skills in this area will have a trickle-down effect, improving your health, motivation, productivity, and general happiness.

1. Know your relationship value.

Often when we don't feel confident in a relationship, we assume we don't have many desirable qualities to bring to the relationship. We look to the other person to define our value and reinforce that we're "good enough" to be in the relationship. In dating situations, you might focus on your flaws and feel insecure about them. But you have many positive qualities you can offer another person. If you aren't aware of those qualities, or if you choose not to focus on them, then you're sending a signal to those you want to attract that you don't feel valuable enough to be in the relationship.

Action Steps: Mentally visualize gathering up all of your flaws and putting them in a big box. Then visualize putting a lock on the box so you can't access it. Now that your flaws are out of the way, you can only focus on your good qualities. Write down everything positive about yourself that you can offer in a relationship. Spend some time on this, and even ask a close friend or family member to share what they see as your positive qualities. Place this list where you can see it daily.

2. Have a relationship vision.

Whether you've been in a long relationship or just beginning one, you may not have a vision for what you'd like from the relationship and how you want it to feel. What kind of communication style would you like? How do you want to resolve conflict? How much time do you want to spend together? How important is physical touch and affection? Without defining this vision, you and your partner are simply reacting to circumstances rather than creating the ideal relationship you want. If you aren't in a relationship now, it's still smart to create your own relationship vision for the future. Then you'll be prepared to find the type of person who will share your vision.

Action Steps: Make a list of relationship questions like those above. You can use the relationship questions at the end of this book to help you. Write down your answers to the questions listed, thinking carefully about the mutual happiness and satisfaction of both people in the relationship. If you are currently married or in a serious relationship, do this exercise with your partner. If you are single, write the answers for yourself and hold on to them for the future when you are in a relationship.

3. Determine your personal boundaries.

It's hard to be confident in a relationship when you have no boundaries. Sometimes we avoid boundaries because we aren't confident. We fear the person we care about will leave us or get angry if we stand up for ourselves or have needs. Does this sound familiar to you? Solid boundaries reflect confidence and increase the respect of those around you. They are necessary not only for the health of the relationship, but also for your own self-esteem. Setting and enforcing boundaries, even if it makes others upset or angry, will give you a huge boost of confidence, because you have the self-respect to know what you want and to require others to respect your wishes.

Action Steps: Think about how you've been allowing others to take advantage of you and how you might be accepting situations that are really unacceptable to you. How is this impacting your relationship? Make a list of things your partner (or other people in your life) may no longer do to you, say to you, or do around you. Decide how you need physical and emotional space. Then set a meeting to communicate this calmly, kindly, but firmly.

4. Notice people pleasing.

People pleasing is the desire to make others happy (or prevent their anger) at your own expense. You feel so uncomfortable with conflict or disappointing others that you're willing to do just about anything to avoid it. You're addicted to the approval and good feelings that come from making people happy and comfortable, as you tend to their needs over your own. It makes you feel validated and worthy. Over time you begin to lose confidence in yourself, because you've lost sight of who you are, what you want in the relationship, or how to live your life on your own terms.

Action Steps: If you recognize yourself as a people pleaser and see how it's harming your relationship, then it's past time to do something about it. This week, choose one situation with your partner or another person you please where you stand up for yourself, say no, or make your own decision—even if it causes conflict. Remain strong. Don't give in even if you encounter anger or withdrawal by your partner. Resist the need to over-explain yourself or to over-apologize for your decision. If necessary, leave the room or hang up the phone until he/she calms down.

5. Focus on the positive.

Quite often we lose confidence in ourselves or in the relationship because we're hyper-focused on the negative. We only see our flaws and weaknesses and fear our partner will reject us as a result. Or we only see our partner's flaws and believe the relationship is doomed. Maybe we've had bad relationships in the past, and the memory of those infects our thinking about our current relationship. However, reality is rarely as negative as we perceive it to be. It might appear negative because that's all we focus on.

Action Steps: Refer back to the list of positive qualities you bring to your relationship. Then make a list of all of the valuable qualities of your partner and what you love about him/her, as well as a list of the ways your partner is better for you than any previous bad relationships. Finally make a list of all of the wonderful aspects of your relationship. Keep this list handy for times when negative thoughts about your relationship creep back in.

6. Act "as if."

Sometimes it takes a while for our feelings to catch up with our thoughts and actions. We might begin thinking positively and have a vision for how we want our relationship to be, but we still *feel* uncomfortable about ourselves and our value in the relationship. If you're single, you might still have low confidence about your ability to attract a partner in spite of your best efforts to think otherwise. While you are waiting for your feelings to catch up with your new awareness and positive thoughts, begin to act "as if" you are confident about yourself and your relationship (or your potential for being in a relationship).

Action Steps: Define where you feel the least amount of confidence related to your romantic relationship. Write down how you believe a confident person would behave in this same situation. Mentally visualize yourself behaving confidently in this situation, and the next time it occurs, play the part of a confident you. Act until you truly feel it.

7. Be aware of clinginess and guilt-tripping.

One of the hallmarks of low confidence in a relationship is clinginess and insecurity. When you aren't confident, you compensate by seeking reinforcement and subtly manipulating the other person through neediness and guilt. You fear they may leave you, so you hold on tighter—which ultimately pushes them away and sabotages your self-respect. Maybe you have legitimate reasons to feel insecure, but holding on tighter or shaming your partner won't fix the problem. Only healthy, open, and confident communication will help you address any real issues.

Action Steps: Think of ways you might be clinging through neediness and guilt. Write down some of the specific things you do that might be passive-aggressive, whiny, or controlling. With the awareness that this behavior isn't healthy for the relationship, write a commitment to yourself to mindfully release one or more of these behaviors this week. If you feel there's a real reason to feel insecure based on your partner's behavior or words, then calmly and maturely communicate your concerns, even if you fear you'll hear something you don't want to hear. Ultimately, you must have honesty and truth as the foundation for any healthy and lasting relationship.

8. Reframe rejection.

Everyone has been rejected by a romantic partner or love interest at some point in their lives. When you open yourself up to connecting with another person, you make yourself vulnerable to possible rejection. Of course rejection hurts, but it is something you can and should move past if you want to enjoy a loving, healthy relationship in the future. Rejection isn't an indictment of your character or who you are as a person. It simply means you and this particular person weren't the right match. In many ways, rejection is a gift, as it saves you from investing any more time in a relationship that won't serve you well. Rejection can be a great teacher, helping you learn more about yourself and what you want and need from another person. Rejection does require a period of grief, but you will move past this grief more quickly when you release blaming, acrimony, or self-criticism, and have gratitude for what the relationship offered you.

Action Steps: Think about past romantic rejections you've experienced. What did you learn about yourself as a result? What lessons did you learn for the next relationship? How have you grown as a result of experiencing the rejection? Visualize a future with this person, knowing they were not the right match for you. Silently express gratitude to them for letting you go and visualize yourself releasing them from your life.

9. Learn relationship communication skills.

One of the foundations of a confident and healthy relationship is communication. When you are able to articulate your feelings, fears, and concerns in an honest and kind way, the relationship can flourish and grow. This vulnerability and authenticity is necessary for both people to feel safe and fully accepted—without fear of judgment, abandonment, or betrayal. When we don't communicate our needs and discuss our differences honestly and freely, intimacy will inevitably break down. Healthy communication also requires active listening with your full attention and an open mind. The most successful, intimate relationships involve proactive communication before a fight ever breaks out. However, conflict is inevitable, and conflict resolution should include collaborative problem solving and a mutual commitment to resolution without bitterness and recrimination.

Action Steps: Even if you think your communication skills are good, it never hurts to fine tune them to make you feel more confident and empowered in your relationship and to maintain intimacy and trust. Sit down with your partner, and ask each other the relationship questions listed at the end of this book to open dialog and understanding. Consider reading a relationship communication book like *Non-Violent Communication: A Language of Life* by Marshall B. Rosenberg or *Getting the Love You Want* by Harville Hendrix. Make a commitment to learn about healthy relationship communication and practice what you learn with your partner.

10. Build sexual confidence.

People who are confident and skilled in romance and sex generally feel good about themselves. They aren't overly self-conscious about their bodies or worried about appearing desirable. However, they do inquire and care about how to please their partner romantically and sexually. They create time for romance and physical intimacy, and they don't blame themselves or their partner when sex doesn't go smoothly. Confident people want stay physically attractive for their partner—but without obsessing about their bodies. Sexual confidence is not all about sex. It is about intimate emotional connection, sharing, pleasing yourself and your partner, and having fun.

Action Steps: Sexual confidence begins with feeling good about yourself and liking who you are. If you're lacking self-esteem, the best place to start is by working to improve it, perhaps through counseling. If your self-esteem is good, but you just aren't confident in the bedroom, remember confident sexual behavior can be learned with education from expert sources and books written by qualified therapists. Do some research and reading to enhance your knowledge and creativity. If you want feel better about your body image, exercise regularly, as the endorphin boost will make you feel great. Also communicate with your partner to learn what she/he likes and share what you like to eliminate guesswork and frustration. This will make you both feel more secure.

Barrie Davenport

Social Life

*"Even in social life, you will never make a good impression
on other people until you stop thinking about
what sort of impression you're making."*

~ C. S. Lewis

Lack of social confidence is a common problem. Nearly half of all
Americans claim to be shy, and nearly fifteen million Americans
have social anxiety disorder, where they experience intense,
persistent and irrational fear of social or performance situations.
Wherever you may fall on the scale of discomfort in social
situations, the problem makes it difficult to develop romantic
relationships, make new friends, or interact with work associates.

A healthy social life is not only critical to your happiness and
confidence, it's also key to your health and longevity. Many
studies suggest social relationships are just vital to your health as
other common risk factors like smoking, being sedentary or
obesity. According to research gathered by Brigham Young
University, people with strong family and social connections have
a 50 percent lower risk of dying over a certain period than do the
non-social group.

When you lack confidence in social situations, it's frustrating to
hear these statistics. It feels as though you're trapped in your fears

and self-doubts, with no ability to change a situation that can add to your health and happiness. In fact, most shy people desperately want to have a social life. They just don't know how to escape from the feelings holding them back. However, it is possible to boost your confidence in social settings and feel more secure about who you are and how you appear to others.

11. Identify anxieties.

Your lack of social confidence can manifest in many ways. Maybe you don't feel comfortable meeting new people. Maybe you feel shy walking up to a group and joining in. It could be really hard for you to ask someone for a date or to call a friend and suggest going out. Some people are comfortable in certain social settings, but fear speaking out at work or in a meeting. Knowing exactly what makes you uncomfortable or anxious is the first step toward correcting the problem. Often we're so steeped in fear and avoidance, we haven't taken the time to identify the specific cause.

Action Steps: Think about the situations or scenarios where you feel least comfortable socially. What exactly triggers these feelings? Where are you and what are you doing? What are the feelings or physical symptoms you experience in these situations? Just identifying these will give you awareness of the issue and where it holds you back

12. Make a social plan.

Once you are aware of the social situations that cause anxiety or discomfort, you can take control of the situation by initiating small and manageable actions to build up your confidence and retrain yourself to enjoy social interactions. Having a plan of action will give you an immediate boost of confidence and make you feel more in control of your emotions. Planned exposure to the situations that cause your discomfort will eventually cure you of your anxious feelings so you can look forward to social interactions and actually have fun.

Action Steps: Think of a social activity you would like to enjoy but that causes you discomfort. Begin with the situation that causes you the most difficulty and attack it first. Plan ahead for how you will enter the room, a few things you will say to people, how many people you will talk to, and how long you will stay. Give yourself permission to leave after the amount of time you committed to yourself. You will feel discomfort the first few times you initiate your plan. But each time, talk to a few more people and stay a bit longer. You'll notice you feel more confident with every social event.

13. Practice a conversation.

For any skill you learn, practice increases your confidence. With repetitive practice, you know exactly what needs to be changed and adjusted, and it allows you to hone your skills until you feel proficient. The skills involved in social confidence require practice as well, and this includes practicing conversation skills. One of the biggest concerns about meeting new people or participating in group conversation is not knowing what to say or fearing you'll embarrass yourself. But with some pre-planning and practice, you'll be armed with plenty of conversation topics and the assurance to initiate a chat.

Action Steps: Before you attend a social gathering, a date, or even an outing with a friend, think about what you want to say when you first arrive. Practice greeting people in front of a mirror, and think about a few topics of conversation you want to initiate as you converse with people. Have some basic, everyday conversation starters (the weather, a recent news story, their family or a mutual friend), and also prepare some interesting questions or observations to initiate a more meaningful conversation. Write some of the topics down to keep in your pocket or purse to refer to at the event if you forget.

14. Notice the voice in your head.

Negative self-talk is universal with those who feel uncomfortable socially. You spend time wondering what others are thinking, how you look to them, and how they might be judging you. You mentally repeat self-criticisms or linger on how fearful and shy you are. People who lack confidence overestimate the negative perceptions of others in social situations. They become paralyzed by their negative thoughts and further isolate themselves, adding another heap of self-criticism and negativity on top of the initial feelings. Of course, none of these negative thoughts help you feel more comfortable or confident. In fact, they just reinforce feelings of self-doubt and anxiety.

Action Steps: Write down all of the fears and false perceptions your mental voice is telling you. Then for each fear, ask yourself, "Is this 100 percent true? How often has this really happened?" Then notice if there is any real evidence to support your negative thought. More than likely, there isn't any or it's greatly exaggerated. In fact, there is probably more evidence that negates these self-critical thoughts. Teach yourself to stop believing your thoughts. Simply notice them without giving them credibility.

15. Practice mirroring.

There is a neuron in the brain that is responsible for recognition of faces and facial expressions. This neuron triggers you to copy facial expression you see on others. You mirror their expressions unconsciously. When you mirror someone's body language you are offering nonverbal cues that you relate to them and feel the same as they do. In fact, research shows people who share the same emotions are likely to experience stronger levels of trust, connection and empathy. You can reverse-engineer this process to make close connections with others by mirroring their expressions and body language.

Action Steps: The next time you converse with someone, practice a mirroring them for a few moments. Don't exaggerate it, but subtly mirror their facial expressions and body movements. Try this with a family member or close friend at first until you get the hang of the subtleties of mirroring. (You don't want to look like you're mocking the other person.) Take note of how they respond to you and whether or not you see them warming to you and the conversation.

16. Learn active listening.

Listening is one of the most important confidence skills you can have. Confident communication isn't just about talking, it's about listening deeply to others. By becoming a better listener, you can improve and enhance your relationships and social interactions, as well as your ability to influence, persuade and negotiate. Active listening involves making a conscious effort to hear beyond just the words the other person is saying. It's mindfully paying attention to the complete message being sent, and being fully focused on the other person without succumbing to distractions.

Action Steps: Practice active listening with a close friend or family member. Give them attention without checking your phone, glancing over their shoulder at someone else, or looking at your watch. Notice the speaker's body language and practice mirroring. Use your body language to show you're listening by nodding and smiling appropriately. Offer feedback and thoughtful comments. The positive response you get from the speaker will make you feel more confident in your communication skills.

17. Understand the art of small talk.

Small talk is the polite and sometimes meaningless conversation you have at parties and other social gatherings. It's light, casual conversation that creates a friendly atmosphere. The skill of making small talk is important in social and business settings, and it shows you have manners, poise and can engage other people. It is a cornerstone of civility, as it fosters contact and encourages kindness. For some people, small talk flows naturally—but for others, making small talk feels tedious and overwhelming. Many people think small talk is an innate talent, but it is an acquired skill. There is a structure and rules for making small talk that makes connecting with others less intimidating.

Action Steps: In your next social encounter, begin small talk by letting the other person know you are willing to engage. Comment on the weather or about something in the surroundings. Then move on to personal introductions and sharing information about who you are and what you do. Throw out a light topic for conversation (a movie, a book you're reading, etc.) and respond back to any topics thrown your way. Try not to spend too much time focused on your favorite topic. Ask questions and show interest in the other person.

18. Notice nervous habits.

Your lack of confidence can show itself in some distracting and unattractive ways. Nervous habits like biting your nails, hair-twirling, clearing your throat, constant twitching or foot shaking, or popping your knuckles, can be irritating to others and suggest you don't feel self-assured or comfortable. Sometimes these behaviors are the result of boredom, but those observing you will perceive you as uncomfortable and nervous. Many of these habits are unsanitary and even unhealthy and make you look silly or childish.

Action Steps: Think about some of the nervous behaviors you have that are habitual. What are some of the triggers for these behaviors in social situations? What are you feeling when you turn to these habits? Discomfort? Boredom? Stress? By noticing the feelings, you will take some of the power away from the emotion, making it less tempting to perform the bad habit. Come up with some positive replacement behaviors to use when you notice you want to perform a nervous habit. For example, when you want to bite your nails, put your hands in your pockets or hold them together in front of you.

19. Practice openness and vulnerability.

When you don't feel confident about yourself or your relationship skills, it is difficult to open up to another person. Often we build walls and shut down emotions in order to protect ourselves from embarrassment or rejection. Vulnerability feels deeply uncomfortable when we aren't sure if something negative might follow. But authenticity is the only path to a real connection in any relationship. You can't close off parts of yourself and feel confident in who you are. When you are reserved and self-conscious, you are depriving others of the benefit of your true personality and uniqueness. You also deprive yourself of the potential for an enjoyable, real connection.

Action Steps: Consider how you might be closing yourself off or being inauthentic in your relationships. Start by taking one small step toward authenticity and vulnerability. Share a life-long dream or talk about an insecurity in a conversation with a friend or acquaintance. Practice speaking from the heart, even at the risk of appearing less-than-perfect. You'll find others relate to you better and find you more approachable.

20. Gain perspective.

Although you may feel highly self-conscious in social situations, the reality is that others aren't paying nearly as much attention to you as you fear they are. Most people are far more concerned with themselves and how they look and sound. Even though you may be filled with doubt about yourself, your appearance, your personality, or your abilities, everyone has some of these same self-doubts. More importantly, everyone has flaws and imperfections. You may not notice them because you're so focused on your own.

Action Steps: Close your eyes for a moment, and mentally acknowledge the fact that your fears and self-doubts are out of proportion with reality. Recognize that others aren't focused on your flaws or assessing you constantly. Remind yourself of this fact when you are in your next social situation.

Career

*"I am not a product of my circumstances.
I am a product of my decisions."*

~ Stephen Covey

Your career is a huge part of your life. If you work full-time, you spend nearly half of your waking hours on the job. How you feel about your career impacts your happiness and quality of life in all areas. If you're unhappy or unfulfilled in your work, your feelings will eventually impact your confidence in your ability to be successful, useful, and productive.

If you have a career you like, but you don't have confidence in yourself or your skills on the job, this will undermine your opportunities for promotions, better jobs within your field, or winning new clients. When you lack confidence at work, you aren't as likely to accept challenging projects, initiate ideas, or speak up in meetings. As a result, others begin to view you as less capable or intelligent and come to expect less from you.

Even though you might be highly-skilled and very bright, the fallout from your lack of confidence will make you question yourself further, as you fail to impress your peers and decision-makers. Over time, your self-esteem takes a hit because your inability to reach your career goals makes you doubt yourself and your worth to the organization. If you lack confidence in yourself on the job, the best thing you can do for your overall happiness and financial success is to work on rebuilding it.

21. Know your career goals.

Often a lack of confidence stems from not being clear on what you want and where you want to go with your career. This uncertainty and lack of clarity makes you hesitant to take risks or boldly seize opportunities. If you don't feel happy or passionate in your work and don't have a vision for your professional future, the odds are good you'll settle for the status quo and never move ahead. You'll feel paralyzed by doubt and lack of direction.

Action Steps: Start thinking about your professional vision and what you want to achieve in the coming years. Do you have a passion that can translate into a career? What are your career goals for the next year, five years, ten years? Start writing this vision and defining your goals. When you do this exercise, suspend logic and pragmatic thinking and allow yourself to think big.

22. Get clear on expectations.

If you don't know what your boss or organization expects from you, you'll always feel on rocky footing and insecure about your performance. Perhaps your boss hasn't communicated these expectations clearly, but it's up to you to find out and drill down to the specifics tasks and results required. Having this definitive knowledge will give you clarity and make you feel more confident in your efforts.

Action Steps: Review your job description and duties if you have access to them. Set up a meeting with your boss to review and discuss his/her specific expectations. If your company has a vision or mission statement, review it to ensure your work aligns with the company mission.

23. Identify weaknesses or opportunities.

Although it's never fun to acknowledge our weaknesses and areas of growth opportunity, you must be clear on *where* you need to improve in order to improve. You likely know some of these weaknesses already, but it's important to know how your boss and decision-makers in your organization view them and where they want you to grow.

Action Steps: Make a list of your perceived weaknesses in your job. Ask your boss where he believes you need to improve. What are some specific actions you can take in these areas to become better? Write them down and create an action calendar for implementing them.

24. Think outside of the box.

Innovators and creative thinkers often get the most attention in an organization. Even though you might feel unsure of yourself, consider new and different ways you can complete a project, save the company money, or come up with a solution to a problem. Rather than following the same routines or the expected method, think outside of the box and impress your boss with your initiative and creativity.

Action Steps: Consider an upcoming project or a regular task in your job. How could you improve, streamline, or recreate it? How can you show your boss and the powers that be the ways in which your ideas will benefit them or the organization?

25. Prepare thoroughly.

Nothing supports confidence more than thorough preparation. Whether you're conducting a meeting, giving a speech, or presenting to a client, when you know your stuff, you feel on top of your game and self-assured. Demand excellence from yourself in your work. Go above and beyond what needs to be done. Give yourself plenty of time and over-prepare. Even if you aren't a comfortable speaker or presenter, your thorough knowledge and command of the subject will make you feel more secure and impress others.

Action Steps: What is the next presentation, meeting, or project you have ahead of you? What do you need to do to feel thoroughly prepared and completely informed? Write down all of the specific steps and create a plan of action working backward from the event date. If necessary, rehearse what you will say and how you'll present the information.

26. Speak out in meetings.

When you lack confidence at work, it feels uncomfortable and intimidating to speak up in meetings. You fear saying the wrong thing, looking stupid, or drawing attention to yourself. However, your willingness and initiative to talk in meetings, share ideas, and argue a point in front of others is a critical factor decision makers consider when it's time to offer a promotion or a juicy project. Sitting silently makes you appear disengaged and disinterested, and will make it more likely you get passed over or ignored.

Action Steps: When is the next group meeting you must attend at work? Find out more about this meeting and the topics that will be covered. What ideas or relevant information can you share during the meeting? Think about exactly what you can say, how you will say it, and when the appropriate time will be during the meeting to bring it up. How can you politely insert your comment into the conversation if you aren't called upon to speak?

27. Box up past failures.

When we make a mistake or experience a public failure in our work, it takes a huge toll on self-confidence. Failure is embarrassing and creates a lot of anxiety about our potential for success and abilities. However, failure also is a sign that you're willing to stretch yourself and take action. The most confident and successful people have had many mistakes and past failures— because they've pushed themselves to take a risk, make a decision, and move forward. Failures give you information you can use for future efforts. Once you learn from failure, don't allow it to remain in your awareness or hold you back. Accept failure as a stepping stone to success.

Action Steps: What past mistakes or failures remain in your thoughts and undermine your confidence? Write down each one, and consider what you learned from them. How has this information helped you or guided you in other efforts at work? What positive changes have you made as a result of this failure? Write downyour thoughts.

28. Find a mentor.

A mentor is a more knowledgeable, experienced person who takes an interest in you and your success. Mentors inspire and motivate you to stretch yourself and do your best work. With a mentor, you can drill down to the emotions, complications, frustrations, and potential roadblocks and get real-world feedback on how to manage these things. Mentors might see something in you that you haven't recognized or acknowledged in yourself and shine a light of awareness on it for you.

Action Steps: Think about successful, accomplished people you know and admire in your office or your field. What do they do that you would like to emulate ? What could you learn from them if you had the opportunity? Make an initial contact with a potential mentor to let them know why you respect them. Invite them to lunch or offer your assistance so you have the chance to observe and talk with them. Remember to respect your mentor's time and express gratitude for their help and support.

29. Dress for the job you want.

Ultimately, what kind of job do you want? Take a look at your mentor, your boss, your boss's boss. What are they wearing? How are they dressed differently from the rest of the staff? If you're a stock clerk, maybe it's time to get out of jeans and a t-shirt and start dressing like a manager. Appearances do count. You'll feel more confident, and people will begin to view you differently when you dress for the success you intend to create.

Action Steps: Go back to your career goals and remind yourself what you want for the future. What career or position do you want? Begin to dress and groom yourself for the position. Look the part until you actually play it.

30. Highlight your strengths.

It's important to acknowledge and work on your weak points, but it's even more important for your confidence and career success to highlight your strengths. Most people have some level of confidence around what they do well. When you build on those strengths and make them even better, your confidence will follow.

It's much easier to strengthen your strengths than it is to improve your weak areas. Become an expert or highly proficient in your strengths, and others will come to respect and depend on your knowledge and expertise.

Action Steps: What is a career strength you posses that is essential to your job? How could you improve this area to become even more knowledgeable? What are the exact steps you need to take to strengthen this strength? Write a list of these steps and plot them on a calendar for action.

Communication

*"Take advantage of every opportunity to
practice your communication skills
so that when important occasions arise,
you will have the gift, the style,
the sharpness, the clarity, and the
emotions to affect other people."*

~ Jim Rohn

Every relationship you have is impacted by your ability—or
inability—to communicate well. Whether at work, in your love life,
or with friends and family, good communication fosters better
understanding, helps us resolve differences, promotes mutual
trust and respect, and allows creative ideas to flourish.

Although communication seems fairly simple and straightforward,
so much of our communication is misunderstood or
misinterpreted. This can cause conflict and wounded feelings in
personal and professional relationships, which undermines our
peace of mind and confidence.

Think about the times you've said something to your spouse or a
friend, and your meaning was entirely misconstrued. Or consider
an occasion when someone said something that hurt your
feelings, only to learn later they had no idea how their words

impacted you. In my own life, I've seen how the power of words can sow the seeds of trust and love—and how they can be divisive, hurtful, or misunderstood.

It's not just the content of your communication that matters. How you speak, and how you look and act while speaking, creates a strong impression on others and lets them know how confident you feel and how capable you are. Having good communication skills is particularly important at work, as your ability to present ideas and share information verbally impacts your success and financial future.

One of the most positive things you can do for your confidence is to learn the skills of healthy, confident communication in your personal and professional life and to put those skills into practice. You'll see how your confidence increases in direct proportion to your ability to communicate well.

31. Be aware of mumbling.

Have you ever listened to someone, and you had to strain to understand what they were saying? They speak so softly or have such poor enunciation you constantly ask them to repeat themselves. Maybe you've noticed other people frequently say to you, "Can you repeat that?" If you're a mumbler, you probably know it. Mumbling can become a bad habit that sends one loud and clear message—"I'm not confident enough to speak clearly and with authority." It also might suggest you really don't want the listener to hear what you say. Either way, it undermines your credibility.

Action Steps: Just the awareness you mumble is a good start toward breaking the habit. To reinforce your awareness, practice speaking in front of a mirror and exaggerate the enunciation and articulation of the words you're speaking. As you speak, open your mouth very wide and pronounce each syllable separately. Keep your voice level modulated and clear, without trailing off at the end of a sentence. Practice this for a few minutes in the morning and evening.

32. Notice conversation fillers.

Conversation fillers are those little sounds like, "um," "er," and "ah," that we use when trying to think of the next thing we want to say. Sometimes we use them because we're nervous and our thoughts escape us. A conversation, presentation, or speech littered with fillers makes the speaker appear unprepared or disengaged. The more you use them, the more dependent you become on them to bridge the gap in your thoughts and words.

Action Steps: Start to notice how often you use fillers in everyday conversation. Begin to catch yourself using these sounds, and mindfully replace them with a deep breath instead. A few moments of silence is far more powerful than filler words, and the deep breath will calm you and allow you to gather your thoughts.

33. Pay attention to pitch, tone, and speed.

Have you ever encountered someone whose voice is really annoying? They talk with a high pitch, speak too loudly, or talk so fast you miss most of what they're saying. The pitch of your voice does make an impact on those who hear you, and they make value judgments based on how you sound. Speaking in a high voice gives the impression you're nervous and lack confidence. A lower pitched voice tends to be calming and persuasive. When you speak too quickly, people can't understand you and begin to tune out and stop listening.

Action Steps: Record yourself reading a few paragraphs from a book. Listen to your pitch and how you modulate it. You don't have to keep a steady pitch all the time—some words and phrases should be voiced in a higher pitch for emphasis. Pay attention to your speed and how loudly you are speaking. As you listen to your voice and practice making corrections, a new way of speaking will come naturally.

34. Think before you speak.

When you're nervous or lack confidence, you can sometimes lose the filter between your brain and mouth. You blurt things out without thinking them through. Or you might be in a rush to "say it and get it over with" before you lose your nerve. By considering and organizing your thoughts in advance, you can save yourself embarrassment or prevent offending someone else. It will also help you share your information more accurately and concisely. When you don't rush to respond or offer an opinion to quickly, you also give the impression of being measured and truthful in your words.

Action Steps: In your next conversation at work or during a more in-depth conversation in your personal life, take a few deep breaths before you respond or comment. Think about what is on the tip of your tongue and whether or not it's what you really want to say. Does your response require more thought? Is your comment accurate? Will your words offend or wound the person or people listening?

35. Stop extraneous movements.

When you speak, do you click your pen, adjust your glasses, or make nervous hand gestures? Whether you're talking in a personal conversation or making a speech, these nervous movements are distracting and reveal any discomfort you're feeling. Appropriate, well-timed hand gestures when you speak can make you look and feel more confident, but often people have no idea what to do with their hands when they speak. They resort to crossing their arms, playing with a prop, or repeating the same hand gestures over and over.

Action Steps: Start to notice what you do with your hands when you're speaking to others. Just this awareness will help you eliminate distracting gestures. If you don't know what to do with your hands, create a neutral position by bending your elbows, with your hands slightly above your elbows and fingertips touching or clasped loosely in a hand clapping position.

36. Speak authentically.

In personal or professional settings, you can't feel confident if your words aren't reflecting who you really are. If you're posturing, pretending to be someone you aren't, or using unnecessary jargon or language that's too formal (or informal) for the setting, then others will view you as inauthentic and unapproachable. The most confident people feel free to be themselves, to allow their personalities and even their emotions to shine through in their speech within the context of the setting. A person who is real and authentic is naturally attractive, more believable, and sets others at ease.

Action Steps: The next time you speak in a group or one-on-one setting, remind yourself to be yourself and reveal your natural qualities. Resist the temptation to converse the way you think you "should" speak or to try to impress with pretense. Let go of trying to be perfect. Take a deep breath, relax, and speak conversationally, as you would with a friend. Natural authenticity is your goal.

37. Use humor.

Humor is a great way to diffuse tension and anxiety for yourself and those around you. It's hard to be funny when you aren't feeling confident, but all of us have been in funny situations or seen something amusing in a video, movie, or on TV. Sharing these stories or drawing out your listeners to share something funny themselves is a great way to lighten the conversation and connect the group. With practice, you can find ways to add levity into your conversations by tapping into your own natural sense of humor.

Action Steps: Think about a recent humorous event or situation you experienced or heard about. Practice verbalizing the story in front of the mirror or share it with one or two people you feel comfortable around. Have a couple of funny stories in your mind and ready for the next time you're in a group. Just be sure the story is appropriate for the listeners!

38. Pay attention to nonverbal cues.

The people who listen as you speak provide great feedback on your confidence and communication skills through their own body language. Do they look like they're attentively listening and making eye contact, or are they distracted and disengaged? Are they smiling, or do they look annoyed? Are they leaning in or trying to back away? Do they seem confused, angry, or frustrated, or do you sense they appreciate and understand your message? You can use these nonverbal cues to adjust your message, delivery, and style when speaking in order to improve your communication in the future.

Action Steps: Pay careful attention to the nonverbal cues others provide when you communicate with them. Watch out for any patterns you see consistently and begin to adjust your speaking skills accordingly. If you can accept constructive comments, ask listeners who are giving negative cues how you can improve your speaking style and message. This will help you to see more positive reactions from others which will give you a huge booster shot of confidence.

39. Practice breathing.

In nearly any situation, mindful diaphragmatic breathing can help calm you and restore energy. Also, abdominal breathing fills the lower lobes of the lungs, and it massages the abdominal organs by the movements of the diaphragm. When you feel anxiety about communicating, conscious breathing can be the refreshing pause that allows you to regain your confidence and poise and calm your nerves.

Action Steps: Become aware of your own breathing style. Is it shallow breathing from the chest or deep breathing through the abdomen? Learn the techniques of proper breathing by researching "diaphragmatic breathing" online. Practice these techniques before any gathering, presentation, or speech or whenever you feel nervous or lacking in confidence.

40. Know what you're talking about.

As mentioned earlier, solid preparation is key to feeling confident, especially in communication. Whether you're having a discussion with a friend about politics or making a presentation, you'll feel much more self-assured if you know your facts and have thoroughly prepared. You need to make a worthwhile contribution to a conversation in order to appear (and feel) credible and on top of your game. If you have to communicate something difficult or complicated, be sure you're able to break it down so your listener(s) can understand your message. It's not just a matter of knowing your facts, but also learning how to present them.

Action Steps: Do you have an upcoming conversation or meeting in which you must share information or ideas? How can you thoroughly prepare by mastering the necessary material, as well as adapting your message to the audience? What topics interest you that you might share in conversation? Read and research more about these topics so you feel knowledgeable and confident.

Appearance

*"The best and most beautiful things in the world
cannot be seen or even touched—
they must be felt with the heart."*

~ Helen Keller

One of the main sources of low confidence for nearly everyone relates to appearance. Research has shown women have dozens (sometimes hundreds) of negative thoughts about their bodies and faces in the course of a week. It's no wonder the problem is pervasive, since the current media ideal for women's appearance is achievable by less than two percent of the female population.

Men have similar anxiety about their appearance and resort to compulsive exercise, strict diets, laxatives, and even making themselves sick in order to lose weight or achieve a more toned body. Men often combat their body image issues by overtraining or even indulging in steroid use. A recent TODAY/AOL body image survey found that men worry about their appearance more than they worry about their health, their family, their relationships or professional success.

Although most of the population is average looking compared to the media's standards, everyone still obsesses about obtaining that ideal. Ironically, both men and women find the quality confidence one of the most attractive in the opposite sex. But how can you have this attractive self-confidence if you don't like how you look?

The key to confidence in your appearance is self-acceptance. Acceptance of yourself as you really are – flaws and all – creates a solid psychological platform upon which to develop a positive self image and confidence in the person you are, beyond how you look. Self-acceptance also liberates you from constant worry, comparisons, and negative self-talk.

41. Pay attention to self-talk.

In a Glamour magazine survey on body image, respondents shared their daily thoughts related to looking at their bodies. Some of the self-talk went like this: "You are a fat, worthless pig." "You're too thin. No man is ever going to want you." "Ugly. Big. Gross." The words we say to ourselves create our feelings, and our feelings cement our beliefs. If you constantly berate your appearance and see it as an impediment to your happiness, you will always feel uncomfortable and lacking. The first step toward confidence in your appearance is to cease saying negative words to yourself.

Action Steps: For one day, carry a small notebook or use your phone to track how many times you have a negative thought or anxiety about your appearance. Once you notice how often you have negative self-talk, create a positive statement to replace the negative thoughts when they arise. For example, you could say, "I completely accept myself and my appearance just as I am." Even if it doesn't feel true at first, continue to bump out negative thoughts with a new positive thought.

42. Focus on your best.

If you follow the same action mentioned in step 41, but instead made note of all the times you have *positive* self-talk about your appearance, you'd have a nearly empty notebook. We tend to focus on our flaws and bypass our positive qualities. Some people are genetically predisposed to focus on the negative, but when it comes to our appearance, most of us see our flaws more than our best features. What if you let your flaws fade to the background and allowed those attractive features to move to the forefront of your attention? Focusing on your best is a conscious choice to improve your confidence.

Action Steps: Make a list of everything you like about your appearance—the texture of your hair, your eyes, how you dress, your strong biceps. Ask a close friend or family member what they think your best features are. Write these down and post the list where you usually look in the mirror. Mentally give more power and vibrancy to your best features and visualize them shining out for everyone to see.

43. Improve what you can.

Self-acceptance doesn't mean you shouldn't make positive change when you can, especially if it improves your confidence and self-esteem. Dressing well, wearing make-up properly, and getting an updated haircut will make you more self-assured and reflect to others that you feel good about yourself. If there's something glaring about your appearance that can be easily and affordably managed (a bad scar, problems with your teeth, acne, too much weight, etc.), then by all means take care of it.

Action Steps: Is there anything about your appearance you don't like that can be changed without danger to your health or too much expense? How would it make you feel to change this area of your appearance? What are the first steps in making it happen? Take action this week to begin the process.

44. Remember hygiene and grooming.

Sometimes we feel so bad about ourselves that we stop trying. We believe we're unattractive, overweight, or too flawed to bother with looking our best. When you give up on basic hygiene and grooming, it could be a sign you're not just lacking confidence— your self-esteem is at stake. You might even be sinking into depression. Even if that's not the case, taking care of yourself by keeping your hair clean, your nails trimmed or manicured, your face shaved (if you shave), and your clothes neat and unwrinkled, will give you an immediate boost of self-respect.

Action Steps: Have you stopped taking care of some of your basic hygiene and grooming? Why have you stopped? Are you feeling bad about yourself and depressed, or do you just feel like it's not so important anymore? If you're feeling depressed for more than two weeks, don't wait to see your doctor, as depression is a serious illness. Otherwise, recommit yourself to looking your best every day. What changes can you make with your hygiene and grooming starting today?

45. Dress well.

Styles change by the minute, and what's considered acceptable in one situation might be completely inappropriate in another. The first step in dressing well for any occasion is choosing clothes appropriate for your body type. If you're short or petite, keep things simple and streamlined without too much fuss or fabric that swamps you. If you're overweight, wear darker colors and smaller patterns. What you should wear for a wedding, dinner party, or date could be entirely different than your attire for a business meeting, a casual movie, or a day with friends.

Action Steps: If you're not comfortable deciding on the appropriate clothes for your body or the occasion, do some research online about both. Research and read some articles online about body type and fashion, as well as on how to dress for any occasion. What do you need to change about your wardrobe to compliment your body and match your lifestyle?

46. Use the mirror technique.

When you deny reality or refuse to accept certain aspects of your appearance, then you create a mental block hindering your self-development and growth. You don't have to force yourself to "like" the things about yourself you don't like. The goal is to avoid giving more power to low confidence by denying or harshly judging reality. The mirror technique is effective in helping foster self-acceptance related to your physical appearance and learning to love yourself completely for who and what you are regardless of your flaws.

Action Steps: Stand before a full-length mirror, completely naked, without the use of any complimentary lighting, makeup, etc. As you gaze over your face and body, make note of your feelings and thoughts. You'll find some aspects of your face and body are harder to look at than others. These aspects have acquired such negative power in your mind that they might impact self-esteem and confidence. Take a deep breath and try to focus on the parts of you that cause you pain. Make a conscious effort to overcome the urge to look away. As you focus on these parts, look in the mirror and repeat out loud, "I completely accept and love myself as I am, whatever my imperfections may be." Repeat the statement with meaning and conviction about ten times. It will be hard at first, but with practice you'll become more relaxed, accepting, and comfortable in your own skin.

47. Maintain healthy weight.

Maintaining a healthy weight for your height definitely makes you feel better about your appearance. You fit better into your clothes and feel less self-conscious about your body in general. There are many health benefits to maintaining a healthy weight. Aside from having more energy, having a healthy weight motivates you to work out more, according to recent studies published in *The International Journal of Obesity.* A healthy weight also improves heart health, decreases the risk of breast cancer and diabetes, leads to better sleep, and increases longevity.

Action Steps: Learn what your ideal weight should be based on your height and body frame. Research online to find an ideal weight calculator to help you find your ideal weight. How many pounds overweight (or underweight) are you based on your ideal weight? If you need to lose weight, a healthy amount to lose is about one or two pounds a week. There are 3500 calories in one pound, so you need to either expend or cut out (or a combination of both) 500 calories a day to lose a pound a week. How you can cut back on daily calories and increase movement or exercise every day? If you're underweight, you need to add calories to your diet—but don't skip some amount of daily exercise, as it has so many other health benefits.

48. Exercise.

I can't underestimate the power of exercise for improving your confidence. Exercise boosts endorphins, the chemicals that make your feel happy and euphoric. It reduces stress and anxiety, lifts depression, boosts brainpower and memory, combats a variety of health conditions and diseases, controls weight, improves your sex life, and promotes better sleep. According to a University of Florida study, people with a poor self-perception boosted their confidence simply by committing to a regular exercise program.

Action Steps: If you aren't exercising at all or just exercising sporadically, you need to make a mental commitment to daily exercise as part of your life—no excuses. It is so important to your confidence and health, it simply cannot be ignored. If you start small and build slowly, you can create an exercise habit that is fun and injury free. Check with your doctor to confirm your fitness level if necessary, and choose an activity you enjoy and that supports your fitness goals (losing weight, building strength, etc.). Determine the optimal amount of time you want to exercise and the best time of day. Begin with just five minutes a day the first week, and perform your exercise immediately after a trigger (an established habit like brushing teeth or looking at email). Build up your time slowly so you allow the activity to form as a habit.

49. Get perspective.

One of the most destructive things we can do to our confidence is compare ourselves to others. We measure ourselves against those who are more attractive and fit, who dress better, who have more hair, and who are younger. We also look at models and actors and wonder why we fall so short of their physical perfection. However, the people we measure ourselves against don't reflect the vast majority of people in the world. Most people are quite average in their appearance and body type. Highly beautiful people represent less than two percent of the population. When you have perspective on the reality of "normal" appearance, you feel more confident you aren't the exception. You are better able to accept yourself and those things about your face and body you don't like.

Action Steps: The next time you are out in a crowd of people, begin to notice the appearance of the people around you. Count the number of exceptionally attractive people. Do this in a variety of settings over time. Unless you work for modeling agency or a Hollywood production company, you'll see how few people meet societal standards of beauty. Remind yourself of this every time you find yourself demeaning your physical flaws or feeling self-conscious about your appearance.

50. Avoid media.

The media is a propaganda machine when it comes to our perceptions of attractiveness. Newscasters are stylishly coiffed with perfectly symmetrical features and shiny white teeth. Magazine covers are adorned with stick thin models who've been airbrushed to perfection. Advertisements celebrate extremely young people with flawless skin and glossy hair, wearing elegant clothes and looking bored. Rarely does the media portray anything "real"—unless it's a tabloid trying to catch a movie star without make-up or with a few extra pounds.

Action Steps: If you suffer with low confidence related to your appearance, do yourself a favor and stop following the media. Don't pick up beauty or style magazines. Get your news from the web rather than TV. Avoid programs that promote an unhealthy focus on appearance, fashion, or weight. Instead, find programs that feature real people doing important, meaningful work or living inspiring lives.

Self-Improvement

"Every man has in himself a continent of undiscovered character. Happy is he who acts as the Columbus to his own soul."

~ Sir J. Stephen

Recently a friend proudly announced she never reads self-improvement books or blogs. "Why do I need someone else to tell me how to live my life? I know how to live my life," she countered when I suggested many of these books actually provide transformative information. She is a practical, no-nonsense person who feels that no one is better at solving her problems than she is.

There is certainly truth to her opinion. Ultimately it is up to each of us to make the changes and take the actions for improving our lives. There's also truth to her assertion that a certain type of "touchy-feely" person (her words) reads self-help materials more than other types of people. I've actually noticed that myself.

If you look at the 16 Myers Briggs personality types, it appears the types with the NF (intuitive, feeling) functions tend to be more inclined toward self-reflection, self-improvement, truth seeking, and other pursuits for inner growth and positive change. But as a touchy-feely type myself, I think *everyone* can benefit from personal growth reading and study, as well as improvement through continued learning, goal setting, and conscious change—even the non-NF types (maybe especially the non-NF types!).

Those not inclined toward self-examination may never realize something needs fixing until it is broken (like a relationship problem, getting fired from a job, sinking into a depression). Sometimes the areas where we are weakest are the places we need to focus the most attention. It is through a desire to become a better, more actualized person mentally, physically, and emotionally, that we feel increasingly confident in ourselves.

As valuable as introspection and learning are to self-improvement, at some point you have to get your nose out of the book or blog and actually do something. It's one thing to have an "ah ha" moment but quite another to transform that moment into an actionable strategy for life change. (That's where our practical non-NF friends might come in handy!) You can't just sit on your enlightened butt. As the old African proverb reminds, "When you pray, move your feet."

51. Learn a new skill.

Whether you enroll in a course, read a new book, or take up meditation, lifelong learning has measurable benefits from the very moment you begin. Learning a new skill, especially a challenging skill you're unfamiliar with, can improve your mental acuity, advance your career opportunities, and boost your confidence. Through continued learning, you develop deeper understanding and breadth of knowledge in areas that interest you. There are certain skills important for career confidence that can be transferred to any workplace—like computer knowledge, troubleshooting, and even public speaking. The Rush Memory and Aging Project reveals that increased mental activity in the elderly slows their decline in cognitive function and makes them less likely to develop Alzheimer's and dementia.

Action Steps: Write a list of several skills you've entertained or even attempted in the past related to your career, a hobby, fitness, or a general interest. As you review the list, think about which skill would afford you the most confidence if you master it. If that particular skill is doable for you now, then write down all of the actions you need to take to start learning it. If it isn't realistic to pursue this skill now, then choose another one. Determine the time of day you'll work on the skill, and begin working on it. Start with a small increment of time (five minutes) if that's possible, so it's easy and effortless initially. Slowly increase the amount of time spent on the skill.

52. Do something creative.

In its obvious applications, creativity is expressed through visual art, writing, dance, and music. Creativity also can be expressed in the most mundane pursuits by finding new and imaginative ways to accomplish a task, tackle a project, or unravel a problem. Anyone can be creative—you don't have to an artist or craftsman. You simply need to step off the beaten track. Practicing creativity floods your psyche with confidence, as you discover the depths of your imagination. Creativity has many other healthy benefits as well. In a 2010 review in the *American Journal of Public Health,* researchers detail how creativity can reduce stress and anxiety, increase positive emotions, and reduce the likelihood of depression.

Action Steps: Consider ways you can practice creativity in your daily life and work. How can you think differently or approach a situation from a new direction? Challenge yourself to let go of the old way of doing things and open your mind to new possibilities. Allow yourself to explore some traditional creative pursuits like writing, painting, photography, or music. Rather than judging or comparing your efforts, just get in the flow of the activity. Enjoy the process without worrying about the outcome.

53. Improve your EQ.

Your EQ is your emotional intelligence quotient. It is made up of four core skills: self-awareness, self-management, social awareness, and relationship management. There isn't a connection between IQ and emotional intelligence, and you can't predict EQ based on how smart someone is. Emotional intelligence is a flexible set of skills you can acquire and improve with practice. When we boost our EQ, we improve our interactions and relationships in all settings. In work settings, emotional intelligence has been proven to be the strongest predictor of performance. A higher EQ affords more self-control, helps you navigate conflict, and makes you a better communicator. All of these outcomes build your confidence, as you see the positive results of a sharpened EQ.

Action Steps: You can begin improving your EQ by first learning your current emotional intelligence score. Find an EQ assessment online and take it. Once you review your results, identify areas where you need to improve your EQ. Read some articles on ways to improve your emotional intelligence, and begin with one skill to focus on for the next four to six weeks. For example, you might work on your reactions during conflict or better understanding your strengths and weaknesses. Put a rubber band on your wrist or use some other cue to remind you of the new behaviors or reactions you're working on.

54. Search for your passion.

Finding work or even a side gig that you love is a huge boost to your confidence. Your passion infuses your life with purpose, meaning, and fulfillment. It allows you to express your innate talents in a way that supports and honors your values, while providing a wellspring of joy and satisfaction. When you pursue your passion, you work almost effortlessly, and because you're so engaged in what you're doing, success comes easily. You become an expert more quickly because you're not expending energy resisting something you don't like. Following your passion creates opportunities and opens doors for new ventures that can upgrade all aspects of your life.

Action Steps: Finding your passion takes time and patience, but even the process of finding it can boost your confidence. Simply knowing you're working toward a career you love or a hobby you enjoy will stir up excitement and anticipation. Carve out an hour a day or every other day to work on uncovering your passion. To help you with the steps of discovering it, check out my *Path to Passion Course* (http://pathtopassioncourse.com/).

55. Set goals.

There's no doubt that setting goals increases your chance of success and the frequency of your success. Setting a goal is the first and most important step toward any achievement. The individual Action Steps to accomplish the goal are the catalyst to turn the inert goal into something dynamic and real. Both the actions toward and the achievement of your goal will boost your confidence. With every step forward, you feel empowered and motivated to continue. With every accomplishment, you'll believe more and more in your capacity for success.

Action Steps: If you don't have clearly defined goals for your personal and professional life, then right now is the best time to create them. Your goals should support your core values, so as you develop your goals, be sure you review your values in the process. Begin with some big yearly goals you want to achieve. Make sure they are SMART goals—specific, measurable, assignable, realistic, and time-related. Break down big goals into smaller goals, and create Action Steps to accomplish over the coming days, weeks, and months. Consider finding a coach or accountability partner to help you stay on track.

56. Break some bad habits.

Our bad habits not only impact confidence, but also they can deplete our self-respect. We know these habits aren't good for us—maybe they harm our health, relationships, career success, or financial security. The resulting problems further weaken our confidence. Bad habits are hard to break, especially habits bound in a physical addiction, like smoking. They involve much more than desire and willpower. Once you learn the skills involved in breaking bad habits, you'll get an immediate confidence boost knowing you finally have the tools to drop the habit. Once the habit is gone, you'll see a cascade of improvements in other areas of your life, catapulting your confidence even further.

Action Steps: Make a list of the bad habits you'd like to quit. Which of these habits weakens your confidence the most? This is the first place to start. If the habits impact you equally, just pick one. It's important to work on one bad habit at a time, because as I mentioned, quitting habits is very difficult, and you don't want to feel overwhelmed. It involves grooving new neural pathways in your brain through the repetition of replacing the bad habit with a positive habit.

57. Read personal growth books.

There are thousands of books on personal growth, and many of them are among the best-selling books of all time. This genre is popular among book readers for a reason. Personal growth and self-help books have transformed the lives of millions of people around the world—motivating, inspiring, and teaching concepts and strategies for self-awareness, confidence, and emotional intelligence. You're reading one right now! Reading these books isn't a substitute for action, but they can inspire action and support the reader in taking steps to improve their lives. As you gain knowledge and awareness through reading, you're empowered to meet challenging situations on your own, which in itself fosters confidence.

Action Steps: You are taking the step right now by reading this book—but in what other areas of your life do you need awareness, knowledge, or inspiration? What part of your inner life do you wish to improve? Once you know that, visit the best-sellers lists in different categories on Amazon, or Google "best-selling books for (fill in the blank—'creating habits,' 'getting motivated,' etc.)." Read the reviews of the book, look at the chapter headings, and read the free pages offered by Amazon to see if the book appeals to you. As you read, take notes or use a highlighter to remember ideas or information that resonates with you.

58. Find a coach or counselor

A personal or business coach helps you make radical improvements in your life or work by inspiring discovery and insight, and encouraging bold action and accountability. A coach also helps you gain clarity and reach your desired outcome faster than you would alone by helping you stay focused and on-track. Professional counselors or therapists work with clients to help them overcome various psychological and behavioral issues using talk therapy. They work with people to improve their sense of well- being, alleviate feelings of distress and resolve crises. Both coaches and counselors support confidence building as they work with you to reach goals, overcome issues, and meet challenges with courage.

Action Steps: Conduct some additional research on coaching and counseling to determine the kind of support that is best for you and your specific goals or life difficulties. You can learn more about my coaching work here, and you can find a psychologist in your area through the American Psychological Associate web site or through your insurance provider. Set a phone appointment to talk with the coach or counselor to see if they are a good fit for you.

59. Know your values.

Your core values are your defining life principles. It's essential to your confidence to know your values and to do whatever you can to align your life with them. Living in harmony with your values creates the fertile environment for confidence and contentment. They help you clarify what is most important in your work and life, and provide a navigation system for making big decisions, finding your life passion, and living authentically. Defining your core values also enhances self-awareness, improves your relationships, and helps you set and achieve your goals.

Action Steps: Set aside time to consider what your values are both for your personal and professional life. Search online for "list of value words" to help you find just the right words. Circle all of the words that could be a possible value. Then reduce the list to your top five for your personal and professional life. Once you have your lists refined, compare your values to your current life. How are you living in opposition to your values, and what can you do to realign your life and values? Write a list of changes you need to make, and identify the change that will immediately improve your confidence to work on first.

60. Define your integrity.

Integrity is a value, and even if you haven't listed it as a core value, it's one you must embrace if you want to have confidence and self-respect. Integrity reflects your consistent commitment to your values, morals, principles, standards, and the behaviors that reflect those. These behaviors include honesty, reliability, and loyalty, as well as consideration of others and tolerance of differences; personal responsibility; fairness; kindness and compassion; and citizenship. If you haven't fully defined what integrity means in your life, or if you are living outside of your integrity, you will feel bad and lose self-respect. It also can negatively impact your career and your relationships.

Action Steps: A good place to start is by noticing where you have feelings of guilt, regret, or remorse. What caused those feelings, and what would you change if you had to do it over again? What have you done to rectify these situations? Look again at the behaviors of integrity (honesty, reliability, and loyalty, as well as consideration of others and tolerance of differences; personal responsibility; fairness; kindness and compassion; and citizenship) to see where you need to define or improve your integrity.

61. Create life balance

Having a balanced life means you manage the various elements in your life without feeling your heart or mind tugged in any specific direction. You have found a system for creating priorities and boundaries based on your values and goals, and have taken action to design your life around this system. More often than not, you feel calm, centered, clear-headed, and motivated. You know exactly how much time you want to devote to work, family, learning, tasks, friends, free time, and other important elements of your life. You understand the value of physical, mental, and emotional balance as well, and create ways to find balance in these aspects of your life as well. Having balance reduces stress and confusion, and frees you up to pursue those priorities that support your confidence and well-being.

Action Steps: Create a vision of a balanced life for yourself. Write down your life priorities based on your values and goals. How is your current life unbalanced based on your ideal? What exactly do you need to shift, delegate, change, or release in order to create this balance? Choose one change this week to implement as you work toward a more balanced life.

Body Language

"I speak two languages, Body and English."

~ Mae West

Stop reading for a moment, and notice how you are sitting or standing. Where are your arms? What is the expression on your face? If someone were to walk in the room right now, what preconceptions might they make about you simply based on your body language?

If you don't think your body has a language of its own, think again. A large percentage of communication and how people perceive you comes from body language. This includes posture, gestures, facial expressions, and eye movements. Your body language might reveal your true feelings or intentions. Perhaps you feel tired, angry, bored, frustrated, or enthusiastic, but some of these might not be feelings you want to communicate in a given situation. Do you really want your boss to know his speech is making your eyes glaze over?

Understanding and managing body language boosts your confidence in two ways. First, by managing your body language and sending appropriate signals in specific situations, you receive positive feedback and feel assured you aren't sabotaging your own success or the perceptions of others.

More importantly, when you practice powerful, positive body language, you're sending messages to your brain to reinforce positive, confident feelings. Confident body language actually makes you feel more confident.

62. Practice smiling.

Smiling not only makes you more attractive and trustworthy, it also improves your health, your stress level, and your feelings about yourself. Smiling slows the heart and relaxes the body, and it releases endorphins that counteract and diminish stress hormones. It also has been shown to increase productivity while performing tasks. According to several studies, smiling can trick your brain into feeling happy, even when you feel sad as you're smiling.

Action Steps: When you wake up in the morning, stand in front of your mirror and smile at yourself. Yes, you will feel foolish, but practice smiling to yourself for a minute or two. When you're in your car or alone at your desk, practice smiling. Be aware of the impact smiling has on other people, and remind yourself to smile more often with others.

63. Pay attention to posture.

You practice good posture when your position sitting or standing creates the least amount of strain on supporting muscles and ligaments. When you sit, your back is straight, your rear is against the back of the chair, your feet are flat on the floor, and you bend your knees at a right angle. When standing you should be able to draw an imaginary straight line from your earlobe through your shoulder, hip, knee and the middle of your ankle. Good posture is essential for avoiding back and neck pain, prevention muscle aches, and keeping your bones and joints in proper alignment. It opens airways to ensure proper breathing, which allows all of your organs and tissues to function properly. Good posture also reflects a confident demeanor to others. When you stand straight, with your shoulders back and head held high, you look self-assured and poised.

Action Steps: Notice your posture right now, as you are reading this book. Are you slumped in your chair with your back bent, neck forward, and shoulders hunched? Practice sitting and standing with correct posture. Look at yourself in the mirror and make adjustments so you feel the proper alignment of your body. Wear a rubber band on your wrist or some other physical reminder to stand or sit up straight. Ask a family member to notice your posture and comment when it's bad. When you enter a room of people or a meeting, correct your posture before you walk in the room.

64. Use power poses.

Social psychologist Amy Cuddy revealed in her 2012 TED talk that standing or sitting with certain poses for as little two minutes raises testosterone levels and lowers cortisol (the stress hormone). These poses can impact your performance, as well as your success at work, with clients, and in your relationships. Many of the poses involve opening your body and taking up space, making you feel more confident and powerful. Says Cuddy, "Our research has broad implications for people who suffer from feelings of powerlessness and low self-esteem due to their hierarchical rank or lack of resources."

Action Steps: Search online and watch Amy Cuddy's TED talk on body language. Make note of the various power poses she explains. You can also look online to find images of people in these poses. Select two or three poses that you might practice by yourself and in professional situations when you want to appear and feel powerful. Practice doing these poses every day for a few weeks until they feel natural.

65. Use engaged body language.

If you want to reach an agreement, win the girl, persuade someone to your side of things, engaged body language gives you more confidence and sends powerful messages to others to win them over. Engaged body language involves using open gestures, smiling and nodding, and mirroring the expressions and movements of the other person. Once you've reached your goal, seal the deal by offering a firm handshake, saying "thank you", and using good posture.

Action Steps: Think about upcoming situations in which you want to reach an agreement or win someone over. Practice the encounter beforehand using engaged body language. In casual conversation, practice mirroring expressions and movements so you feel confident with it before your big meeting.

66. Remember your arms and legs.

Crossing your arms suggests you feel defensive, self-protective, and closed off. Crossing your legs away from another person can suggest you dislike them or feel discomfort. Crossing your ankles can signal you're holding something back and not expressing it (unless you're a woman who was taught to do this as a "ladylike" position).If you clasp your hands behind your back, you might be saying you feel bored, anxious, or even angry. Hands clasped and crossed over the genitals is a self comfort gesture that reveals vulnerability or shyness. Tapping your fingers and fidgeting tells others you are bored, impatient, or frustrated.

Action Steps: Begin to pay attention to what you do with your arms and legs in certain situations. Notice how you are feeling when your arms and/or legs are crossed. What is the other person saying or doing, and why might you feel defensive or closed off? Begin to change the position of your arms and legs. Put your hands in your lap when sitting and by your side when standing. Crossing your legs at the knee for comfort is fine, as long as it's not combined with crossed arms.

67. Have a strong handshake.

A firm, sold handshake is a universal sign of confidence, and everyone, including women, should have one. A handshake should be strong, but not crushing, offered with a cool dry hand and a few up and down shakes, as well as a few seconds of eye contact. It is a sign of mutual respect from both parties and makes a great first impression. A sweaty, limp, "dead fish" handshake has the opposite effect. Whether or not you feel confident, a firm handshake will boost your feelings and make others see you as more confident.

Action Steps: Ask several people you trust to assess your handshake. Have them make note of your grip, the feeling of your palms, whether you pump their hand appropriately, and if you make eye contact. Make note of their feedback, and practice your revised handshake with people you don't know.

68. Dress for confidence.

In a 2012 study published in the *Journal of Experimental Social Psychology,* subjects who wore doctors' lab coats scored higher on attention-related tasks than did those who did not. Clothes do make a difference in how we perceive ourselves, and how others perceive us. Dressing confidently is more than wearing the trendiest fashion. It's about feeling good, looking poised and being self-assured in all situations. It's also about sending the right message to the people you are with. You can boost your confidence about yourself and your attire when you dress appropriately for the occasion, know the audience, reflect your personal style, and understand the impact of color.

Action Steps: Does your wardrobe add to your confidence or diminish it? Do you often find yourself in sloppy clothing or not dressed appropriately for the situation? Dressing well will add to your confidence, even when you are feeling down. Determine your personal style by looking at magazines or blogs to see what you like. If necessary, purchase a few classic pieces to add to your wardrobe that make you feel confident and powerful.

69. Stop fidgeting.

Over 500 managers surveyed by Adecco USA, a workforce solutions company, said that one fifth of the candidates they've rejected for a position were fidgeters. They felt it betrayed a lack of confidence and a lack of preparation for the interview. Fidgeting, like twirling your hair, shaking your foot, or biting your nails, is an obvious sign of anxiety and nervousness. These nervous movements draw attention away from what you're saying and distract people from your message. Avoid touching your face or neck which also indicates you feel anxious. Fidgeting sends the message loud and clear that you aren't self-assured.

Action Steps: Do you have some regular fidgeting habits? Have others commented on these behaviors in the past? Start to pay attention to how you fidget and what triggers these actions. Think about what you can do to replace these nervous habits when you encounter the trigger. You could hold your hands in your lap, use your hands to gesticulate when you speak, or hold a pen and pad.

If you shake your foot or knee, place both feet flat on the floor. When you feel the urge to fidget and have nervous energy, take a few deep, calming breaths.

70. Practice appropriate eye contact.

Eye contact suggests you're truthful, engaging, and approachable. It imparts a sense of intimacy and confidence to your interactions, and makes the other person feel more positive and connected to you. However, too much eye contact can send the signal you're aggressive or maybe even a little strange. When eye contact goes from gazing to staring, it makes people uncomfortable and actually activates their sympathetic nervous system. According to Michael Ellsberg, author of *The Power of Eye Contact*, "In order for eye contact to feel good, one person cannot impose his visual will on another; it is a shared experience."

Action Steps: If you feel uncomfortable making eye contact, start to get comfortable by practicing with family and friends. Look them in the eye for about 50–60 percent of the conversation ideally. When you break eye contact, look to the side rather than down. Looking down signals lower-status, shame, and/or submission. As you get more confident with eye contact with family and friends, practice it with people at work or out in public.

Thinking

"Begin challenging your own assumptions.
Your assumptions are your windows on the world.
Scrub them off every once in awhile, or the light won't come in."

~ Alan Alda

Changing your thoughts is the most essential aspect of boosting your confidence. Your thoughts create your reality. Your thoughts also produce the emotions you have about yourself and your abilities. If you think you're incapable, not smart enough, or lacking in some way, you're flooded with negative feelings that suck your energy and motivation.

Also when you have fearful, diminishing thoughts, all of your other efforts toward building confidence are compromised. These other efforts can help shift your thoughts, but if you are mentally resisting the actions you're taking, the process is slower and more cumbersome.

The optimal way to approach creating confidence is by changing your thoughts and your behavior at the same time, even if you have *feelings* of fear or doubt. By mindfully ceasing old thought patterns and replacing them with new ones, you're teaching your brain new habits and creating new neural pathways. Taking confident action helps solidify your new thoughts, as it provides tangible evidence your thoughts are true and reinforces your mental efforts.

As you shift your thinking about yourself and your confidence, and support that shift with confident actions, you'll notice your emotions will follow suit. You'll feel less and less insecure and anxious, and increasingly self-assured about your capacity for success and happiness.

71. Notice negative thought patterns.

Random thoughts float around in your head like uninvited guests. There's an endless voice chattering away like a monkey about life events, your daily to-do list, or the lunchbox you forgot to give to your child. If you examined your thoughts, you'd see many of them, probably most of them, are negative and self-sabotaging. You dwell on the past, worry about the future, obsess about failures and mistakes, battle shame and guilt, and allow your thoughts to drift into mine shafts of negativity and anger.

Action Steps: Awareness is always the first step toward change. For a few days, mindfully notice your thoughts. This will take some focus, so you may want to post reminders around your house, your car, and your office. Try to notice patterns of negative thinking and the triggers that set off the thoughts. Make notes about these patterns and the topics of your negative thoughts so you don't forget.

72. Practice pattern interrupts.

As you become aware of patterns of negative thinking, your goal is to break the patterns. The more you allow negative thoughts to have free reign in your mind, the stronger and more debilitating they become. Repetitive negative thinking can lead to depression, anxiety, and even physical illness. It can certainly prevent you from being happy, productive, and confident. Beyond just breaking the thought pattern, you want to replace the negative thought with a positive thought. If you leave a void, your brain will automatically return to the negative thinking pattern.

Action Steps: Put a rubber band on your wrist, and every time you notice negative thoughts arising, gently pop the rubber band as a physical pattern interrupt for your brain. Create a positive statement that's the opposite of the negative thought. For example, if your negative thought was, "I'll never finish this project on time," change the thought to, "I have all the time I need to finish the project completely and successfully." Even if you don't believe the new thought initially, say it out loud if possible and to yourself several times. Don't worry if it feels silly or useless. You are taking control of your thoughts and retraining your brain.

73. Replace thought loops with action.

Interrupting negative thoughts and replacing them with positive ones is a powerful tool for change. You can reinforce this practice with action. When you are focused on something that requires mental focus or physical exertion, your brain is occupied with the task at hand. Have you noticed when you're engaged in a project, intently focused on a sport, or doing anything that's challenging, your worries disappear—at least for a while? Action prevents you from getting stuck in negative thought loops, and it has the further advantage of allowing you to do something productive or useful. Taking control of your thoughts, deciding to take action, and accomplishing something useful all add to your confidence.

Action Steps: Plan ahead for this strategy by choosing activities or projects you enjoy that require focus and attention. It could be something creative like cooking, drawing, or playing an instrument, or it could be a work project or household task that is mentally challenging. It needs to require enough focus that your mind doesn't wander to your negative thoughts. When you notice yourself in a negative loop, replace the thought as outlined in #72, and then take action on one of your pre-planned activities. As you practice, your negative thoughts will simply become a trigger for positive thought and action. You might even come to view negative thoughts as your motivator.

74. Challenge limiting beliefs.

Negative thoughts that have had years to percolate in your mind will grow into limiting beliefs. These beliefs might have had some element of truth initially, or they may have no truth at all, but you accepted them as truth because they were implanted so powerfully. Limiting beliefs often go back to childhood experiences, and the pain that accompanies the beliefs makes it very difficult to disengage from them. However, when you challenge these beliefs and shine the light of truth on them, you can begin to loosen the stronghold they have on you and your confidence.

Action Steps: Think about the limiting beliefs you have about yourself. These beliefs often relate to your worthiness, your desirability, your intelligence, your appearance, your personality, or your abilities. In some area of your life, you were told or it was implied you weren't "enough." Write down these limiting beliefs. Then think about the initial source or reason you adopted the belief in the first place. Now think about how the belief is no longer true for you or maybe never was true. Find specific evidence in your life that contradicts the belief. If you can't find the evidence, what could you do to create it now or in the future?

75. Learn to meditate.

Meditation is an approach to training the mind, similar to the way that fitness is an approach to training the body. There are many goals to meditation, but one of the main benefits is the ability to detach from your thoughts, releasing their control over you, and to simply be present in the moment. As you grow in a meditation practice, you'll find it far easier in your daily life to release your thoughts without judgment, thus avoiding many of the negative feelings that accompany the thoughts. Of course, meditation has a myriad of other benefits for your health and well-being, all of which support your efforts toward building your confidence.

Action Steps: Research and read articles online on my site about the benefits of meditation. You'll discover how powerful the practice is and why you should begin a meditation practice. Consider adding meditation as a daily practice. Begin with just five minutes a day immediately after a trigger (an established habit like brushing your teeth). Slowly increase your meditation time each week until you reach your desired time to meditate. Begin to notice how the practice of meditation is impacting your thinking during the day.

76. Practice daily gratitude.

Through the dark cloud of negative thinking, we often fail to see the good in our lives. We don't acknowledge the people, experiences, and successes we've enjoyed in the past and continue to enjoy every day. A variety of studies have proven the power of expressing gratitude and its impact on our happiness, self-esteem, and confidence. A University of California study revealed those who wrote about gratitude were more optimistic and felt better about their lives. They also exercised more and had fewer visits to physicians than the control groups who didn't express gratitude.

Action Steps: Keep a gratitude journal, and every evening before bed write down everything you are grateful for. Think about people in your past or present life who have positively impacted you, and write them a letter expressing your gratitude. Also, write down the benefits you enjoy in your life that you take for granted—enough food, clean water, a comfortable bed for example. Use thoughts of gratitude as replacement thoughts for negative thinking.

77. Develop present moment awareness.

Meditation grounds you in the present moment as you release thoughts and focus on breathing. However, you can't meditate all day. You have responsibilities to take care of and people you want to connect with. However, you can pull one element of meditation to use in your daily life. This element is mindfulness—present moment awareness and engagement. Even when you're engaged in "mindless" activities like doing the dishes or washing the car, you can redirect your attention to the task at hand and find joy and satisfaction in what you're doing. Mindful action and attention trains your brain to stay in the only reality available to us—the present moment.

Action Steps: The practice of mindfulness takes some practice in order to naturally draw your attention to the task at hand. Create a physical reminder for yourself that you'll see frequently (like a rubber band, a ring on a different finger, etc.) so you are prompted to return to the moment and what you are doing. Notice each aspect of the most simple tasks, like the feel of water running, the sounds in the background, and the smells in the room.

78. Practice affirmations.

Affirmations are basically a form of auto-suggestion, and when practiced deliberately and repeatedly, they push the subconscious mind to take action to make the positive statement real. Repeated positive statements help you focus your mind on your aim, as if it is already real. They create corresponding mental images, which affect the subconscious mind accordingly. Affirmations also reinforce chemical pathways in the brain, strengthening neural connections so that our thoughts change the structure and function of our brains to support our intentions.

Action Steps: To practice affirmations, choose one or two to focus on for several weeks. Say the affirmation out loud in a confident voice several times a day and before you go to bed. To add more power to the affirmation, write it down as you speak it. Be sure your affirmations are in the present tense, as though they are a current reality. You can find a list of 101 positive affirmations on my site, Live Bold and Bloom, that you can use, or you can create your own affirmations related to your specific goals.

79. Visualize success.

Visualization is the use of mental imagery to create visions of what we want and the process of making it happen. It is often used by athletes to improve their skills by picturing their optimal performance and ultimate achievement. A variety of studies have offered sufficient reliable evidence that mental imagery can improve motor performance.

With visualization, you create neural patterns in your brain, just as if you had physically performed the action. The thought can stimulate the nervous system in the same way as the physical action does. Visualization fosters better performance and outcomes in all areas of life that require preparedness and forethought.

Action Steps: Determine an upcoming situation or area of performance in which you want to succeed. Set aside time in the morning and evening for a five-minute visualization, as well as in the hours just before the event. Visualize all the images, sounds and feelings in your mind surrounding an activity. Mentally go through each step as if you were performing perfectly, culminating in a successful outcome. Try to feel the feelings of energy, confidence, stamina, or whatever feelings you would produce in a successful endeavor.

80. Focus on compassion.

Cultivating empathy through compassion meditation affects brain regions that make us more sympathetic to other peoples' mental states, according to researchers at the University of Wisconsin-Madison. Brain scans reveal that brain circuits used to detect emotions were dramatically altered in subjects who practiced compassion meditation extensively. Compassion meditation is useful for preventing depression in people who are susceptible to it, and it also reduces stress and improves feelings of happiness, contentment, and self-compassion.

Action Steps: Sit in a comfortable posture in a quiet, peaceful place to meditate. Take several slow, deep, diaphragmatic breaths. Become aware of your mind and body, relaxing any muscle or mental tension that arises. Turn your attention to people you have seen or know who have experienced misfortune. Using your own words, wish them freedom from sorrow or stress and swift recovery to a happier, healthier present and future. Continue offering compassion to any people you may be aware of who are suffering.

Fun and Adventure

"When you have confidence, you can have a lot of fun.
And when you have fun, you can do amazing things."

~ Joe Namath

As adults, our lives are complicated and filled with obligations, worries, and responsibilities. We're involved in the serious business of grown-up stuff. We work hard. We support our families. We worry about our money and higher prices. We fret about the condition of the world, politics, our children. We have endless chores and tasks without much time for fun.

A prolonged period of stress can put your physical and mental health at risk. —but stress is part of everyday life. Sometimes we even wake up stressed, just anticipating the day ahead of us. A long commute to work in traffic; dealing with a difficult boss; having deadlines to meet; and coping with the responsibilities of family and home life all impact our well-being and erode our joy and confidence.

Having confidence does help you manage stress and enjoy life, but you can create the conditions for confidence by first managing stress and creating opportunities for fun and adventure. Studies prove fun and laughter can reduce stress by releasing the feel-good endorphins in your brain.

Incorporating adventure into your fun has further benefits for your confidence, health, and well-being. Adventure travel or outdoor adventure activities force you out of your comfort zone and increase your tolerance for uncertainty. These pursuits also open your mind to new sites, activities, and people. Adventure can stretch you physically, but it can also be a great opportunity to learn more about yourself and what you're capable of. Every time you challenge yourself through an adventure, you gain the confidence to do something even more bold, and that confidence spills over into all areas of your life.

81. Cut back on your to-do list.

It's difficult to add fun and adventure to your life when it's crammed full of activities and obligations. Often we have the mindset we must be busy with something "productive" every minute of the day. The more we have on our plates, the more obligated we feel to keep the plates spinning. However, much of the busyness in our lives is unnecessary. It has nothing to do with our values or our vision for who we want to be and how we want to live. Chronic busyness drains our energy and joy and can even lead to illness and anxiety.

Action Steps: Write a detailed list of all of your daily, weekly, and monthly activities and obligations. How many of the items on the list could you drop without any fallout? Are there any items you feel pressured to keep even though you don't want to? Start cutting back to make room for fun and adventure. This week, pick one activity or task to drop.

82. Simplify your space.

Material things can drain our energy. As we accumulate more and more, we have to spend more time caring for and maintaining these things. Physical clutter creates mental clutter and disharmony, and it brings on fatigue and agitation. As you start to release material things from your life, you have a sense of freedom and peace. It reenergizes you and allows you to reclaim time you could be spending on more productive, interesting, and fun activities.

Action Steps: Pick one room at a time and begin the process of simplifying and decluttering. If you never use something or it serves no useful purpose, then sell it or give it away. If you have clothes you haven't worn in a year, let these go so someone who needs them can take advantage of them. Think about the number of rooms in your home you actually use. How can you simplify the less used rooms to minimize cleaning and upkeep? Do you have cars, boats, or other toys that sit in the garage? Why not sell them and use the money for an adventure?

83. Plan ahead for weekends.

After a long week, we tend to arrive at Friday afternoon with no plans for the weekend. We're tired and mentally drained, so we let Saturday morning roll in with some vague idea of what we might do for fun. But we end up with our fallback activities of cleaning the house, running a few errands, and than watching a little football at the end of the day. Before we know it, the weekend's over, and we feel like our lives are boring and uneventful. You can't have a life of fun and adventure unless you take the time to plan for it.

Action Steps: Sunday afternoons or evenings are great times to plan for the following weekend. Think about the people you want to spend time with and what brings you joy. Plan activities that are not your usual choices. Do something interesting or challenging.

Take a day trip, learn a new sport, or try zip lining. Don't allow weekends to creep up on you without a plan for fun.

84. Do something playful.

When you were a child, play was a natural part of your life. In fact, play was your method for learning, exploring the world, and developing creativity. According the American Academy of Pediatrics, play "contributes to the cognitive, physical, social, and emotional well-being of children and youth." But what happens to play as we get older? Why do we lose our delight in play and a sense of playfulness in our grown-up world? Play is often perceived as unproductive and frivolous—unless it's competitive play. But play is just as important for adults as it is for children. Play is essential for problem-solving, creativity, and relationships. It helps couples form intimacy, and can foster deeper connections with friends and even strangers.

Action Steps: The type of play I'm suggesting isn't competitive or highly structured. It's purposeless, often spontaneous, pleasurable, and fun. Think about how you enjoyed play as a child. Many of the same types of play you gravitated to when you were young might intrigue you as an adult. You might still enjoy drawing, building block towers, or having tickle fights. You might love exploring outside, telling silly jokes, or building a fort. Give yourself permission to enjoy play, and start adding playfulness to your days.

85. Ride a bike.

Riding a bike can be a form of play if you don't approach it competitively. Hopping back on a bike as an adult makes you feel like a kid when you had complete freedom to zip along at lightning speed with no particular agenda. It's fun and wildly liberating.

Cycling also can be a low-impact, aerobic workout that provides a myriad of health benefits and can be continued for life without a major time commitment. A bike is a versatile machine designed to minimize stress and maximize exercise efficiency. It involves less pounding than other forms of exercise like running. It is gentler on joints and can actually strengthen them, as the cycling motion provides nourishment that builds up cartilage.

Action Steps: If it's been a while since you've been on a bike, go to your local bike store for a test ride, or ask to borrow a friend's bike for a quick ride to get comfortable again. Once you have the hang of it, borrow or rent a bike for the day. Find a bike path or trail in your area, pack a lunch and a good book, and enjoy a peaceful ride. You may enjoy it so much you want your own bike.

86. Plan adventure travel

Adventure travel forces you to be a beginner again. No matter how educated, competent, or confident you might be at home, traveling in a foreign country or in an adventurous situation reduces you to someone who is dependent on his or her wits and the kindness of strangers. The more you step out of your comfort zone, the more you accept the challenge of adventure and embrace the unfamiliar, the more your confidence will grow—not just in your ability to navigate a new place, but also in yourself and your capacity to grow as a person. Travel is a perfect laboratory for building confidence by challenging yourself to try new things, push your limits, and intentionally engage with strangers.

Action Steps: When you're lacking confidence, planning an adventurous trip is probably not on the top of your to-do list. This is exactly why you need to plan a trip like this. Consider taking a trip where you engage in a physical adventure, like rock climbing or white water rafting. If that feels like too much, plan a walking trip in a foreign country or check out one of the easier adventure trips or weekend getaways offered by REI Adventure.

87. Join a group.

If adventure travel isn't realistic right now, you can still find ways to enjoy adventure in your own back yard. If you are shy or uncomfortable in groups, joining a social group centered around specific activities is a great way to ease yourself in to a group dynamic through shared interests. Through your local Meet-Ups, social media, or online forums, you'll find a variety of group events for everything from hiking to book clubs. When you join a group, you not only boost your social skills, but also you create opportunities for new friendships, business referrals, and enhanced learning.

Action Steps: Think about some of your favorite interests or activities—or even skills or pursuits you'd like to try for the first time. Do some online research on groups in your area by looking on Facebook, MeetUp, LinkedIn, or simply Google your specific interest and add the words "Atlanta groups or clubs," using the name of your city. Challenge yourself to attend a few meetings to see how you like the group. Just by taking the initiative to go to a group meeting, you're boosting your confidence.

88. Break out of daily routines.

Your daily routines and habits feel very comfortable, and they probably make your life easier and more productive. However, even if your routines are working, there are benefits to shaking things up. Sticking to the same methods month after month puts your brain on autopilot and can make life feel boring and tedious. Any time you force your brain to learn something new, you encourage your brain to create new neural connections. Change forces you to pay more attention to what you're doing and have more present moment awareness. Even small changes like taking a different route to work or switching up the order you do things in the morning can boost your brain power and confidence, and make life more interesting.

Action Steps: How can you shake up your daily routines? What can you do differently to challenge yourself to learn a new method, try a different route, or approach something from an unexpected angle? Pick one area where you can break your routine and apply it this week.

89. Find passionate people.

The quality of our lives and even our confidence is impacted by the people we surround ourselves with. If you are surrounded by people with limited thinking, who are entrenched in the status quo and resistant to change, they will surely limit you. If you have people in your life who diminish you or try to hold you back from success and happiness, you will feel diminished and unhappy. If you want to feel happy, successful, and confident, surround yourself with happy, successful, and confident people. Find people who are enthusiastic and passionate about their lives and work, who are doing interesting things and living adventurous lives. Their excitement and enthusiasm will rub off on you.

Action Steps: Think about people you know or work with who are passionate and enthusiastic. How can you interact with these people and make a real connection with one or more them? Consider hosting a dinner event with interesting people who are involved in various activities and projects that seem adventurous and unique. Begin a search for your passion or a strong interest and join a group where like-minded people hang out. Make a point of finding one new person who can expand you and challenge you to be more passionate yourself.

90. Do the "big thing."

Most people have a bucket list of things they want to do or accomplish before they die. Often there's one "big thing" at the top of the bucket list that keeps calling to us, urging us to go for it, to seize the golden ring. Sadly, most people never accomplish their "big thing" or even cross off many items on their bucket lists. Life and responsibilities get in the way, and we keep pushing off our dream goal, thinking we have endless time to pursue it. One of the top five regrets of dying people is that they left their dreams unfulfilled. By prioritizing your "big thing," you take control of your destiny and honor your dreams, filling you with confidence to pursue anything you desire in the future.

Action Steps: What is your "big thing"? What is one thing you want to do before you die? Grab a pen and paper and calculate the following. Assuming you live to age ninety, how many years do you have left. Subtract your current age from ninety. Now multiply that number by 365, and that's the number of days you have left to live. You don't have an endless supply of days, so isn't today the best day to make sure your "one big thing" happens? What can you do right now to plan your big thing?

Finances

"Money is only a tool. It will take you wherever you wish, but it will not replace you as the driver."

~ Ayn Rand

Low self-confidence is one of the main impediments to financial success. It makes us doubt our abilities and judgment and prevents us from actualizing our potential. One reason confidence is so important is its impact on ambition and motivation. People with a positive attitude who believe in themselves have more ambitious goals, and they regularly act on those goals, leading to more opportunities and higher incomes.

Whether someone is highly-educated and working in a prestigious profession or as a blue-collar employee, confidence has been proven to be a determining factor for making a better income.

However, simply taking control of your financial habits can boost your confidence and improve your financial position. According to a survey by the Certified Financial Planner Board of Standards, Inc., Americans who have a financial plan of any sort feel more confident and are more optimistic about their futures, and they are more likely to save money and have fewer financial difficulties.

Whether or not you are earning a great income or enjoying the career success you aspire to, practicing smart financial habits will give you clarity, put your money to work for you, and place you in the driver's seat of your financial future. As you master your financial goals and habits, you'll feel more confident in all areas of your life.

Confidence will improve your financial situation—and good financial knowledge and planning with improve your confidence.

91. Get organized.

Nothing makes you feel more out-of-control than disorganization. If your financial system involves bills and important documents scattered around the house or stuffed in drawers, it's hard to feel confident about yourself and your skills at money management. Having an organized financial system can save you time and reduce the stress of not being able to put your hands on something when you need it. To get organized, you need to create a workable system to track your financial information—everything from spending to retirement plans. A system will help you pay bills on time, track your expenses, and easily see how your investments are performing.

Action Steps: Begin by gathering all of the paperwork, bills, receipts, and documents you have scattered in various places. Create stacks for each type of paperwork (bills, mortgage document, insurance, etc.), and arrange them by date. Organize these stacked piles into separate file folders or boxes, labeled with what they are. If you have some information or documents on your computer, write a list of all of these. Look online to find a good outline for setting up a basic filing system for all of the documents you've gathered. Consider reducing paper by setting up online bill pay and banking, and learn to use an online personal finance system like Quicken, so you can view all of your accounts in one place.

92. Create a debt payoff plan.

In a culture driven by consumerism, getting into debt can happen without much thought or effort. It's easy to convince ourselves we need the latest and greatest of everything, from iPhones to cars. Our bad spending habits are compounded by high interest rates, making it even harder to stay on top of debt. Having financial debt not only impacts your confidence and financial future, it also can make you sick. According to an Associated Press-AOL Health poll, the stress from being in debt can cause migraines, anxiety, ulcers, severe depression, and even heart attacks.

Action Steps: Paying off debt will require living below your means and perhaps finding other sources of income until the debt is paid. Start with your smallest debt first. It will be the easiest to pay off, and checking this debt off your list will give you a boost of confidence and motivation to tackle the rest. Read some articles by finance expert Dave Ramsey on paying off debt.

93. Find leaks.

If you check your monthly bank statement and wonder where all of your money is going, it might be leaking out in unintentional ways. Often we spend of things we don't really want or need, or we have recurring expenses we've forgotten about and don't use, but we've neglected to cancel them. Money can trickle out of our pockets in a variety of ways, and you might as well light a match to some of your bills if you don't plug the leaks. Finding these leaks is especially important if you're trying to pay off debt.

Action Steps: Begin by tracking your spending for a month. Carry a small notebook, or use your smartphone, and make note of everything you spend. If others in your family are spending as well from the same bank account, ask them to spend on a cash-only basis for a month and give them a set amount of cash. Review any automatic payments on your bank and credit card statements to make sure you aren't being charged for things you no longer want.

94. Streamline your expenses.

In addition to finding leaks in spending, you can save money (or help pay off debt) by consciously streamlining your spending. So much of our spending is unconscious—a few lattes at Starbucks, an impulse purchase at the mall, a few extra grocery items because we shop while hungry. By cutting out these unnecessary purchases, you'll not only save money, but also you'll feel more disciplined and mindful about your spending decisions.

Action Steps: The best way to streamline expenses is by creating a budget. You have some fixed expenses like a mortgage payment, but other expenses can be cut back or eliminated entirely. Review your bank statements and credit card bills to see any expenses you can eliminate from your budget. Determine your budget for variable items like entertainment, travel, food, clothing, etc. Consider a cash-only system for spending on these variable items. Whatever budget you create, be sure it is less than the amount you earn.

95. Learn about investing.

Investing is putting your money to work for you so you can make money from your existing money. People are often intimidated by investing, so they avoid learning or hand off the responsibility to someone else. However, if you don't know anything about investing, you won't feel assured your advisor is doing a good job or if they understand your financial goals. You might not know if you're being charged fairly for financial services or racking up too many investment fees that benefit the broker rather than you. Learning the basics of investing doesn't need to be intimidating—it will give you the confidence to make sound decisions about your investments.

Action Steps: Start by learning some basic terminology of investing by doing some online research. Learn the differences between stocks, bonds, mutual funds and certificates of deposit (CDs). Understand more about compound interest. Research basic financial theories such as portfolio optimization, diversification and market efficiency. Search Amazon to find some basic investing books that are highly rated to help you.

96. Meet with a pro.

Do you have a decent knowledge of investments? Do you enjoy reading and researching about investing? Do you have time to monitor and evaluate an investment portfolio? If you answered "no" to these questions, you'll feel a lot more confident about your investment decisions with the help of a financial advisor. A good advisor will help you understand your financial goals; suggest what to do differently, how much to save, and various types of retirement accounts. They'll advise you on your mortgage, insurance, and taxes. Then they'll create a plan of action with specific steps to achieve your goals. You want to be sure to hire a financial adviser who is required to put your financial interests as a top priority.

Action Steps: Begin looking for a good financial advisor. Look for someone who is a Certified Financial Planner (CFP). This is a significant credential as the advisor must pass a rigorous test administered by the Certified Financial Planner Board of Standards. Ask friends, family, and business associates for referrals for a good CFP. You can also search for a CFP on the

Certified Financial Planner website. Contact the planner, and set up an initial meeting to discuss your financial goals.

97. Define financial freedom.

Financial freedom is more than just having a lot of money. It hinges on living around your values and prioritizing what is most important to you. We often have fear around money tied to our needs for freedom and security. These fears also reveal a belief that money is a scarce resource—there isn't enough to go around. We chase more and more money in an effort to assuage our fears and grab our piece of the pie. A scarcity mindset undermines confidence and cripples our career and financial decisions. The best way to gain financial freedom is to stop being a slave to money. Instead, use your core values as a guide to determine your life priorities. Focus your time, energy, and money on those priorities—even if it means living with less or making less money.

Action Steps: Review your core values. Does your life reflect and support those values? Do you spend most of your time focused on what is most important to you? How much money do you really need in order to live a balanced life centered around your values and priorities? What is the first step you can take to create a lifestyle that reflects your new definition of financial freedom?

98. Create financial goals.

If you don't know where you're going, how are you going to get there? With any life or career achievement, setting goals is the fastest way to success. If you want to achieve or gain something down the road that requires money—whether it's a new car, a college education for your kids, or retirement income—you need to have financial goals with specific actions and a timeframe to reach those goals. Creating and achieving financial goals makes you feel in control of your destiny and more confident in your ability to be disciplined and focused.

Action Steps: What are your short-term (in the next five years) and long-term (ten or more years) financial goals? Write a list of everything you want to achieve or attain that will cost you money. For each list, prioritize those goals. Begin by saving $1000 for an emergency fund, and set an amount you can add to that fund each month. Then move on to the top goal on each list, and determine exactly how you are going to get from where you are now to where you want to be. What is your timeframe for reaching your goal? Break the goal down into small milestones you need to meet weekly, monthly, quarterly, and yearly. Automate any savings or payments you can to remove temptation to spend. Make it difficult to access any money you put toward savings.

99. Involve your spouse/family.

If you have a spouse and family, getting your financial house in order can't be done in isolation. Everyone in the household will be impacted by financial decisions and actions. You must involve your spouse or partner, and even your children when they are old enough to understand concepts around spending and saving. Money is often the biggest source of conflict with married couples, and most arguments center around spending and lifestyle choices. This is why it's so important to determine your core values as a couple and define financial freedom and financial goals for your family. Without this communication and agreement about mutual values and goals, your family will never be on sound financial footing.

Action Steps: Set up a time to meet with your spouse or partner to discuss each person's values and individual goals and dreams. From that discussion, work together to create your top family values, life priorities, and financial goals. Using this information as a guide, work together to determine a debt payment plan, monthly budget, and savings plan. Communicate your family values and priorities with your children, and think of ways they can participate in budgeting and saving.

Conclusion

When you lack confidence in one part of your life, it can feel like you simply aren't a confident person. You paint your entire life with a broad brushstroke of insecurity and doubt. Confidence problems train us to believe untruths about ourselves, and the powerful negative feelings of failure, embarrassment, or shame, make us wary of stepping on a potential emotional land mine. Why tempt fate if it's possible we might fall on our butts once again? We embrace our limiting beliefs as reality.

The feelings of low confidence don't define you or your essential worth. Everyone lacks confidence from time to time, and most people have pockets of insecurities that hold them back in certain parts of their lives. But remember, you don't have to be perfect to be successful, happy, and confident. Confidence is a state of mind that allows you to accept failures and flaws, move past them, and to even learn from them.

Confidence is a skill you can learn, practice, and improve over time, just like any other skill. Brain science has proven repetitive thoughts and actions actually rewire neural pathways to foster measurable change. When you practice confident actions and thoughts repeatedly, *you will* eventually feel confident. As your confidence grows, those pockets of insecurity and self-doubt will shrink and have much less power over your thoughts, emotions, and actions.

If you accept the premise that change is possible, that you can learn the skills of confidence, then begin taking some of the small steps outlined in this book to reinforce your confidence. In manageable increments, expose yourself to the things you fear. Decide on the actions you will take in the next few weeks related to the areas where you lack confidence and commit to yourself and others that you will follow through. Of course you'll feel insecure and uncomfortable at first, but the more you practice these actions, the easier it will become.

As a review, here's how I suggest you use this book to help boost your confidence:

- Read through the entire book once, making notes about any the life areas where you need to work on your confidence.

- Go back through the book again to review those specific life areas you want to work on and the ideas and Action Steps suggested.

- Select the most troublesome area of low confidence to work on first, and determine very specific actions based on the suggestions outlined in the book to work on over the next four to six weeks.

- Determine the time of day you'll work on those actions and a specific trigger or cue to remind yourself to perform the action.

- Expect to feel uncomfortable and resistant for the first few weeks. Try to manage your discomfort by reminding yourself it will diminish over time.

- Seek out accountability and support from a friend or family member by telling them about your confidence work.

- Acknowledge your small daily actions and reward yourself immediately after you take the action with something that makes you feel good.

- Track your feelings of confidence weekly as you work on these actions by scoring yourself from one to ten, with ten being very confident and one being very low confidence. Give yourself a baseline score before you begin taking the actions.

- Repeat this process for any additional areas of low confidence.

You will have times you forget to work on your confidence actions, or you have life disruptions that prevent you from taking the action. There will be days when you feel low and don't believe anything will ever change for you. Please don't use these setbacks as an excuse to quit or to believe "it just isn't working." Stay committed to the work. Affirm to yourself that you are growing more and more confident. Use these affirmations to support your daily efforts. Mentally intend that you are a confident, happy, successful person, and visualize yourself in that position. If you remain committed and diligent, you will notice an improvement in your feelings of confidence. The more you work at it, the stronger those feelings of confidence will be.

You have something valuable and beautiful to offer the world, your community, your friends and family. You have the intelligence, resources, and desire to reach your goals, create success as you define it, and become the person you want to be. You also have the power to build your confidence so you have the motivation and self-belief to make all of these things happen. Don't wait another day to take action. An extraordinary life awaits you.

Relationship Questions

Use this list to help you create relationship confidence with your spouse or partner.

1. What should I never say to you, even in anger or frustration?

2. How much time and space do we need apart from each other?

3. What activities and interests can we develop that will bring us closer?

4. What is going to really set you off?

5. What happens if we can't agree on something important that involves both of us?

6. What kind of physical touch best says "I love you" to you?

7. What could I do that would cause you to pull away from me?

8. How many days between sex will be too long?

9. When you get home from work, what would you like me to do or say in the first few minutes?

10. Who do we know that has the kind of intimacy that we want?

11. What changes will I need to make in order for you to be really happy?

12. Where will we be in this relationship five years from now?

13. What's the biggest lesson I can learn from you?

14. What do you do when you feel hurt by me?

15. What will ruin our relationship?

16. What habits do I have that are upsetting to you?

17. How can we both get our needs met when we want different things on a particular day?

18. What happens if one of us needs more space that the other?

19. What do we do if both of us are having a bad day?

20. How affectionate would you like to be with me?

21. What can we do to avoid fighting or arguing entirely?

22. What about our financial situation might become a recurring problem?

23. What about our work might become a recurring problem?

24. How will we let each other know what we want sexually?

25. What will I have to say to get your attention when I've not been able to?

26. What need of yours have I not been able to satisfy?

27. What kind of memories do we want to create together?

28. What will keep us happily together for years to come?

29. What will be the early warning signs that our relationship is in trouble?

30. How will you be able to forgive me if I've done something that really hurts you?

31. What will you do if you feel tempted by another person?

32. What personality differences do we have that might cause a problem?

33. When we argue, how will you take responsibility for your part of the problem?

34. How can we make our sex life even better?

35. What are your deepest wounds and how can I support you there?

36. Where are you unwilling to compromise?

37. What about my voice or communication style makes you want to spend less time around me?

38. What do you expect from me that you should really be expecting of yourself?

39. What are you willing to do with or for me that you haven't been able to do in previous relationships?

40. What are your deepest dreams and desires for yourself and for us?

Want to Learn More?

If you'd like to learn more about confidence and self-esteem, please visit my blog
Live Bold and Bloom
(http://liveboldandbloom.com/)
for more articles, or check out my online course,
Simple Self-Confidence
(http://simpleselfconfidence.com/).

Did You Like Confidence Hacks?

Thank you so much for purchasing *Confidence Hacks.* I'm honored by the trust you've placed in me and my work by choosing this book to improve your confidence. I truly hope you've enjoyed it and found it useful for your life.

I'd like to ask you for a small favor. Would you please take just a minute to leave a review for this book on Amazon? This feedback will help me continue to write the kind of Kindle books that will best serve you. If you really loved the book, please let me know!

Other Books You Might Enjoy from Barrie Davenport

Confidence Building: Get Motivated, Overcome Social Fear, Be Assertive, and Empower Your Life for Success

Sticky Habits: 6 Simple Steps to Create Good Habits that Stick

The 52-Week Life Passion Project

Made in the USA
Middletown, DE
29 July 2017